SCALES
and
CHORDS

A PROGRESSIVE APPROACH TO LEARNING MAJOR AND MINOR SCALES

WENDY MURPHY FACHINI

Authorunit
Number and Address
877-826-5888
17130 Van Buren Blvd., Ste. 238, Riverside, CA 92504

Because of the dynamic nature of the Internet, any web addresses or links contained in this book may have changed since publication and may no longer be valid. The views expressed in this work are solely those of the author and do not necessarily reflect the views of the publisher, and the publisher hereby disclaims any responsibility for them.

ISBN: 978-1-958895-91-7 (Paperback Edition)
ISBN: 978-1-958895-92-4 (E-book Edition)

Printed in the United States.

CONTENTS

*T*his book is dedicated to my piano teacher Roberta E. Buck, and my son and computer tech consultant, Roger Anthony Fachini III.

INTRODUCTION – HOW TO USE THIS BOOK

The purpose of this book is to provide a series of increasingly difficult scale, chord, and arpeggio exercises, creating a thorough background in Major, Harmonic Minor, and Chromatic Scales. Natural and Melodic minor scales, though not included in all of the exercises, may also be incorporated into music instruction. *Scales and Chords* is designed to be a supplement to any keyboard method of instruction, beginning about level 3 or Early Intermediate level. Most of the examples included in this book will not have fingerings included. The student should be familiar with whole steps, half steps, tetra chords, basic scale and chord fingerings, how to play chromatically, and I- IV- V chord progressions in some of the basic Major and Minor keys. I have included an appendices of scale and chord fingerings, one octave scales and I-IV-I-V-I chord progressions as a reference for all twelve major and minor scales.

Each level of instruction is rather involved. Beginning with Scale Pattern 1 the entire page of exercises is repeated in each key listed in the first exercise. Every time a level is completed, the student begins the next level's exercises back in the key of C Major. The new level is completed in each key listed in the first exercise. Beginning at Scale Pattern 5, the student will study the exercises for that level in all 12 major and 12 minor keys. It will take at least twenty-four weeks to complete each pattern thereafter. I have included a Keyboard Harmony level after Scale Pattern 6. This level gives a break from the general scale work and focuses on the chordal relationships between the keys around the Circle of Fifths

PREFACE

When I began teaching piano back in 1994, I searched for a scale book to supplement my own instruction. As a young student, my teacher, Roberta Buck, gave me a thorough grounding in scales, chords, and arpeggios that I wished to pass on. What I found was a plethora of scale and chord reference books, which, while useful, did not provide progressively more challenging exercises in scale or chord work. This was frustrating as I feel it is important to be comfortable executing scales, chords, and arpeggios. As a result, I began to write out the exercises remembered from my past and created this progressive scale and chords book.

For the past fifteen years, I have used this book in my studio as a supplement to the various methods of instruction available to piano teachers today. It has proved to be an outstanding addition to my curriculum, producing young pianists that execute scales, chord progressions, and arpeggios with ease. They understand that musical structure is built around scales and chords and leave my studio with a thorough grounding in these basic skills.

WHAT IS A MAJOR SCALE?

A major scale is a series of eight notes arranged in a pattern of whole steps and half steps. W W H W W W H, or C D E F G A B C where:

C to D = Whole Step

D to E = Whole Step

E to F = Half Step

F to G =Whole Step

G to A = Whole Step

A to B = Whole Step

B to C = Half Step.

WHAT IS A NATURAL MINOR SCALE?

A natural minor scale is a series of eight notes arranged in a pattern of whole steps and half steps. W H W W H W W, or A B C D E F G A where:

A to B = Whole Step

B to C = Half Step

C to D = Whole Step

D to E = Whole Step

E to F = Half Step

F to G = Whole step

G to A = Whole Step

Every Major Scale has a "relative" natural minor scale with the same key signature. The relative minor of any major scale, begins on the 6th tone of the major scale. You can also count three half steps down and two letter names down from the first note of the major scale. To create a harmonic minor scale, raise the 7th note of the natural minor scale by ½ step. Harmonic minors will be used in this book unless mentioned otherwise.

THE CIRCLE OF FIFTHS

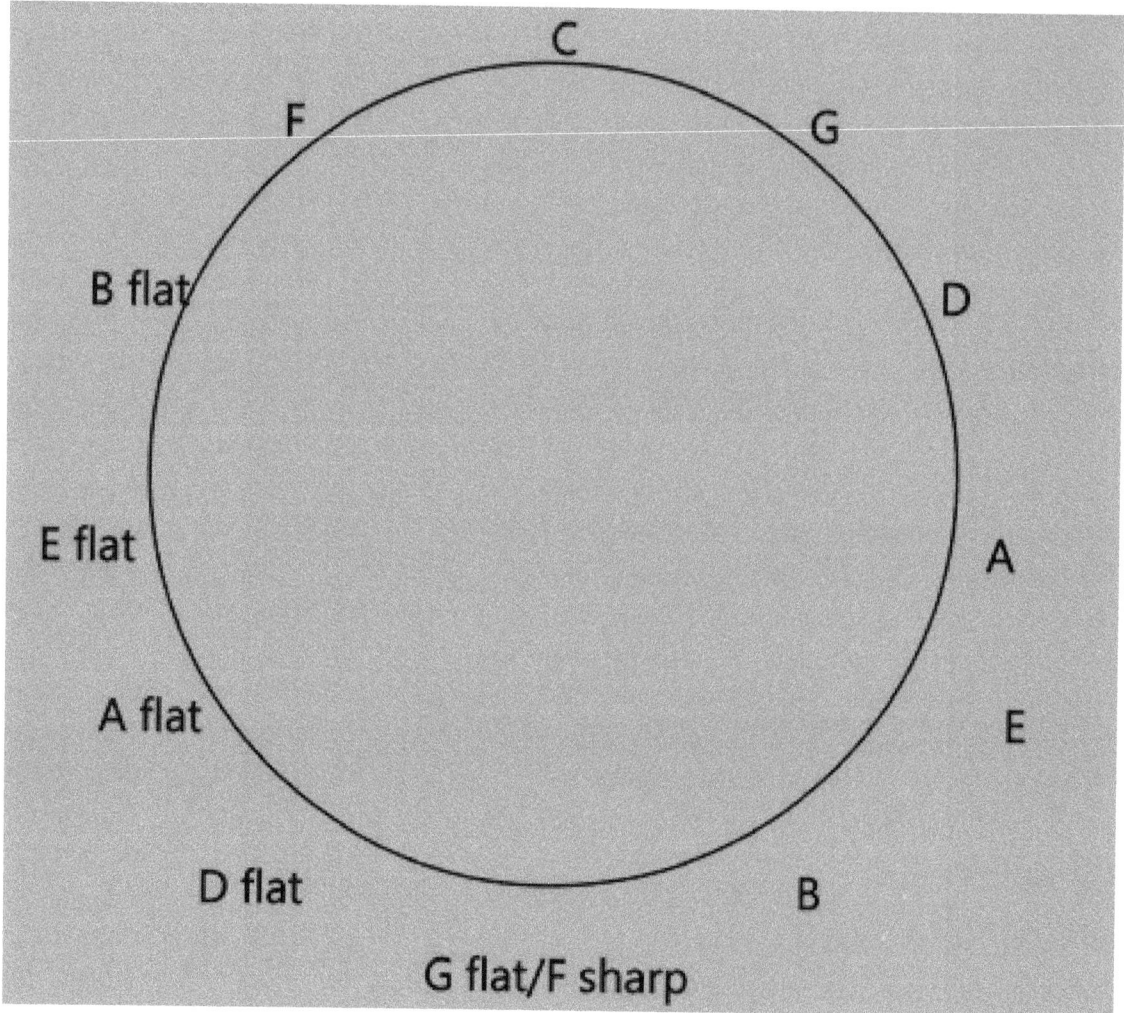

Moving up the keyboard by perfect 5ths beginning on C will take you around the circle of fifths clockwise adding a sharp to the key signature each time. Moving up the keyboard by perfect 4ths beginning on C will take you around the circle counterclockwise adding a flat to the key signature each time. MEMORIZE THIS!

Order of sharps: F C G D A E B

Order of flats: B E A D G C F

PREPARATORY SCALE PATTERN

Before studying major and minor scales, it is best to begin with 5 finger patterns in major and minor keys. The major 5 finger pattern is WWHW and has a "happy" sound. The minor 5 finger pattern is WHWW and has a "sad" sound.

3

SCALE PATTERN 1

1. One octave Major scale hands separate.

C-G-D

Right Hand fingering is 1 2 3 1 2 3 4 5. Left Hand fingering is 5 4 3 2 1 3 2 1.

2. Build a triad on each note of the scale. Play hands separately. Major scale triads on each note of the scale:

Scale degree: I ii iii IV V vi vii I

Chord quality: M m m M M m dim. M

Left Hand fingering is 5 3 1. Right Hand fingering is 1 3 5.

3. Play the following pattern using the Major Scale Triads above. Play LH, RH, LH. RH.

Continue this pattern with all the triads up the scale

4

SCALE PATTERN 2

1. One octave scale, hands separate, then try together.

Major: C-G-D-A-E-F-B flat

Harmonic Minor: a-e-d

2. Play the following pattern building a triad from each note of the scale. Play LH, RH, LH, RH.

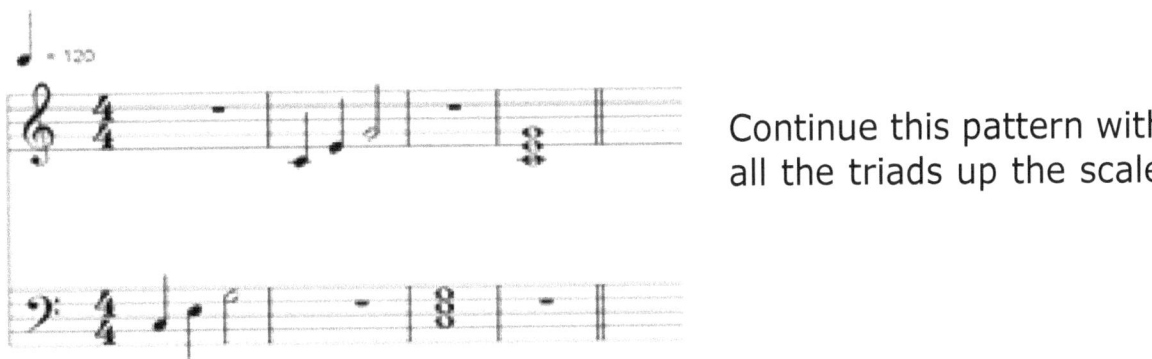

Continue this pattern with all the triads up the scale

3. Play the following pattern using inversions of the I chord.

Left Hand fingerings are 5 3 1, 5 3 1, 5 2 1

Right Hand fingerings are 1 3 5, 1 2 5, 1 3 5

SCALE PATTERN 3

1. One octave scale, hands together.

   Major: C-G-D-A-E-B-F-B flat-E flat-A flat

   Harmonic Minor: a-e-d-b-g

2. Playing a Chromatic Scale (same every week)
   Chromatic Scales use all keys moving by half steps.
   Right Hand fingering begin on D: 1 3 1 2 3 1 3 1 3 1 2 3 1
   Left Hand fingering begin on D: 1 3 2 1 3 1 3 1 3 2 1 3 1

   Play hands alone, together parallel, and together contrary motion.

3. Chord Progressions

   I-IV-I   I-V-I   I-IV-I-V-I

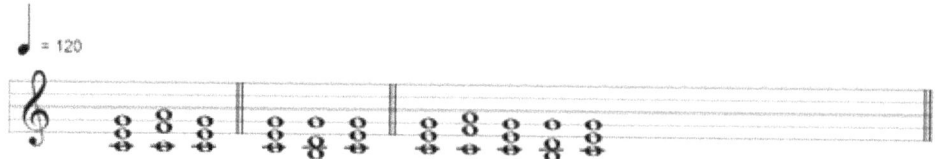

4. Chords: hand over hand – continue pattern up the scale

6

SCALE PATTERN 4

1. Two octave scale, hands together.

    Major: C-G-D-A-E-B-F-B flat-E flat-A flat-D flat-G flat

    Harmonic Minor: a-e-b-d-g-c-f

2. Play one octave scale in contrary motion.

3. Chords: hand over Hand up the scale as in level 3.

4. Chord progression I-IV-I-V-I with inversions. Hands separate, then together.

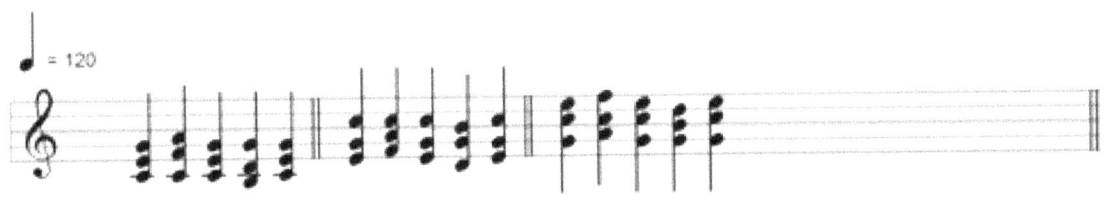

Root position   1st inversion   2nd inversion

5. Chromatic Scale (see level 3) play 2 octaves beginning on D for all weeks on this level.

    Play hands together contrary motion and then parallel motion.

SCALE PATTERN 5

1. Major and minor scales in rhythm, hands separately.

    Major: C-G-D-A-E-B-F-B flat-E flat-A flat-D flat-G flat

    Harmonic Minor: a-e-b-f sharp-c sharp-g sharp-e flat-b flat-f-c-g-d

    One octave –quarter notes

    Two octaves – eighth notes

    Three octaves – triplets

    Four octaves – sixteenth notes

2. Arpeggios- two octaves ascending and descending, hands separate. Line 1 Root position, First Inversion, and Second Inversion.

RH fingering 1 2 3 1 2 3 5 3 2 1 3 2 1; LH 5 4 2 1 4 2 1 2 4 1 2 4 5

3. Chord Progression I-IV-I-V-I / i-iv-i-V-i no inversions, hands together.

4. Chromatic Scale – Four octaves, ascending and descending, beginning on the tonic of your current key, hands separate.

SCALE PATTERN 6

1. All Major and Minor scales, four octaves hands together, ascending legato and descending staccato.
   Major: C-G-D-A-E-B-F-B flat-E flat-A flat-D flat-G flat
   Minor: A-E-B-F sharp-C sharp-G sharp-E FLAT-B FLAT-F-C-G-D

2. All Major and minor arpeggios, four octaves hands separate, on I, IV, and V chord of each scale.

3. Chords, 4 octaves, run hand over hand.

   Majors: I – ii – iii – IV – V – vi – vii/dim - I

   Minors: i – ii/dim– iii/aug – iv – V – VI – vii/dim – i

4. Memorize order of sharps F-C-G-D-A-E-B
   Memorize order of flats B-E-A-D-G-C-F
   Memorize Circle of Fifths forward and backward:
   C-G-D-A-E-B-F sharp-D flat-A flat-E flat-B flat-F

KEYBOARD HARMONY

This level is all about learning Keyboard Mastery, or KM. KM is achieved when the pianist keeps his eyes entirely off the keyboard and on the music. Ideally, one should not need to look down at the keys to play. In these exercises, it is necessary to have memorized the circle of fifths, both in major and minor keys, forwards and backwards.

1. Warm up:

   Run hand over hand I chords chromatically and around the circle of fifths in Major and Minor keys.

2. Play the following pattern of broken and blocked chords in major and minorl keys.

Week 1: Major keys, Week 2: Minor keys
a. **Chromatically**
b. **Clockwise around the circle of fifths**
c. **Counterclockwise around the circle of fifths**

3. Run chords hand over hand around the circle of fifths using I-IV-V chord progression in each key.

   For example, in C, major you would run a C chord, F chord, and G chord. Then moving to the key of G major, you would run a G chord, C chord, and D chord, continuing around the circle of fifths. (C-F-G, G-C-D, D-G-A etc.)

SCALE PATTERN 7

1. All Major and Minor Scales, 4 octaves hands together, ascending pp-ff and descending ff-pp.
   Major: C-G-D-A-E-B-F-B flat-E flat-A flat-D flat-G flat
   Minor: A-E-B-F sharp-C sharp-G sharp-E flat-B flat-F-C-G-D

2. All Major and Minor keys, four octave arpeggio ascending and descending where:
   a. **Root position chord in LH, arpeggio in RH.**
   b. **First Inversion chord in RH, arpeggio in LH.**

3. Extended Authentic Cadence (chord progression)

   I – IV – I – V – V7 - I

4. Chromatic Scale, hands separate, two octaves ascending, one octave descending. Do this 3 times, then descend to original starting note. Begin on the tonic note of your current key. Try hands together.

SCALE PATTERN 8

1. All Major and Minor scales, 2 octaves hands together, from the octave and in thirds (or tenths), in parallel and contrary motion.
   Major: C-G-D-A-E-B-F-B flat-E flat-A flat-D flat-G flat
   Minor: A-E-B-F sharp-C-sharp-G sharp-E flat-B flat-F-C-G-D

2. Broken chord arpeggio, hands separate, pattern 1.
   RH fingering: 1-2-3-5, 1-2-4-5, 1-2-4-5, 1-2-3-5 and reverse for descending.
   LH fingering: 5-4-2-1, 5-4-2-1, 5-3-2-1, 5-4-2-1 and reverse for descending.

3. Chromatic Scale, one octave hands together, parallel and contrary motion from the octave and in thirds or tenths.

4. Octave study, hands separate.

5. Chord Progressions:

   Major: I – ii – vi – IV – ii – V - V7 – I

   Minor: i – ii/dim – VI – iv – ii/dim – V – V7 – i

SCALE PATTERN 9

1. All Major and Minor scales, 4 octaves hands together.
   Major: C-G-D-A-E-B-F-B flat-E flat-A flat-D flat-G flat
   Minor: A-E-B-F sharp-C sharp-G sharp-E flat-B flat- F-C-G-D

2. Arpeggios and scales, two octaves hands separate.
   Ascend arpeggio, descend scale, ascend scale, descend arpeggio.

3. Arpeggios and chords, two octaves hands together.
   Root position chord LH, two octave arpeggio RH.
   First inversion chord RH, two octave arpeggio LH.

4. Arpeggios and chromatic, two octaves hands separate.
   Ascend arpeggio, descend chromatic, ascend chromatic, descend arpeggio.

5. Broken chord arpeggio patterns, hands separate, ascending and descending.

6. Chord Progressions:

   I – IV – V7 – I

   I – I dim – V7 – I

   I – V dim – V7 – I

   I – vi – ii – V7 – I

SCALE PATTERN 10

1. All Major and Minor scales, 4 octaves, hands together.

   Major: C-G-D-A-E-B-F-B flat-E flat-A flat-D flat-G flat
   Minor: A-E-B-F sharp-C sharp-G sharp-E flat-B flat- F-C-G-D

2. Arpeggios, hand over hand, through the chords of the scale.

   Major: I – ii – iii – IV – V – vi – vii/dim – I
   Minor: i – ii/dim – iii/aug – iv – V – VI – vii/dim – i

3. Maj/min 7th, Dim. 7th, Maj 6th, Aug. chord with passing tone.

4. Extended Authentic Cadence and inversions. I – IV – I – V – V7 – I

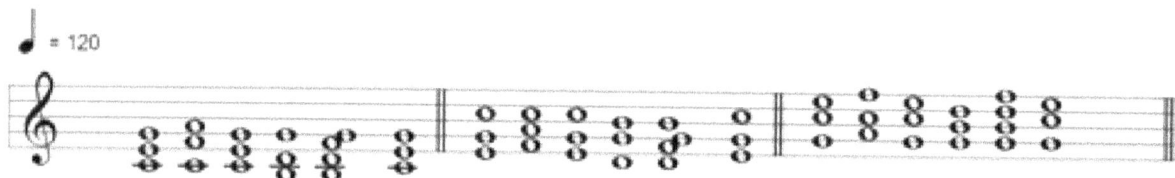

5. Chord Progressions:

   I – V min – V – ii – V7 – I

   I – vi – IV – V7 – I

   I – I dim. – V7 – I

   I – V dim. – V7 – I

SCALE PATTERN 11

1. All Major and Minor scales 2 octaves hands together. Do 2 times.
   a. **LH staccato – RH legato**
   b. **LH legato – RH staccato**
   Major: C-G-D-A-E-B-F-B flat-E flat-A flat-D flat-G flat
   Minor: A-E-B-F sharp-C sharp-G sharp-E flat-B flat- F-C-G-D

2. Arpeggios, root position, hands separate, ascending and descending.
   a. **one octave in quarter notes**
   b. **two octaves in eighth notes**
   c. **three octaves in triplets**
   d. **four octaves in sixteenth notes**

3. Broken chord arpeggio patterns from level 9, hands together.

4. Chromatic Scale, 2 octaves hands separate, as follows:
   Chromatic Scale ascending – Glissando descending
   Glissando ascending – Chromatic Scale descending

5. Chord Progression

   I–IV-I–V–I and inversions
   I–I aug. – I dim–ii–IV–V7–I
   i-i7-IV-iv-i
   I–vi–ii–V7–I

APPENDIX I – ONE OCTAVE SCALE FINGERINGS

C- G- D- A- E major and minor:

RH – 123 12345 / 54321 321
LH – 54321 321 / 123 12345

B (C fl at) major and minor:

RH – 123 12345 / 54321 321
LH – 4321 4321 / 1234 1234

F sharp (G fl at) major:

RH – 234 123 12 / 21 321 432
LH – 4321 321 4 / 4 123 1234

F sharp (G fl at) minor:

RH – 34 123 123 / 321 321 43
LH – 4321 321 4 / 4 123 1234

C sharp (D fl at) major:

RH – 23 1234 12 / 21 4321 32
LH – 321 4321 3 / 3 1234 123

C sharp (D fl at) minor:

RH – 34 123 123 / 321 321 43
LH – 321 4321 3 / 3 1234 123

F major and minor:

RH – 1234 1234 / 4321 4321
LH – 54321 321 / 123 12345

B flat major:

RH – 4 123 1234 / 4321 321 4
LH – 321 4321 3 / 3 1234 123

B flat minor:

RH – 4 123 1234 / 4321 321 4
LH – 21 321 432 / 234 123 12

E flat major:

RH – 3 1234 123 / 321 4321 3
LH – 321 4321 3/ 3 1234 123

E flat minor:

RH – 3 1234 123 / 321 4321 3
LH – 21 4321 32 / 23 1234 12

A flat major and minor:

RH – 34 123 123 / 321 321 43
LH – 321 4321 3 / 3 1234 123

APPENDIX II – CHORD PROGRESSIONS

I-IV-I-V-I chord progression fingering:

RH – Root position: 135, 135, 135, 125, and 135

 First inversion: 125, 135, 125, 135, and 125

 Second inversion: 135, 125, 135, 135, and 135

LH – Root position: 531, 521, 531, 531, and 531

 First inversion: 531, 531, 531, 521, and 531

 Second inversion: 521, 531, 521, 531, and 521

APPENDIX III - CHROMATIC SCALES

Fingering tips:

1. The third finger in each hand will play all the black keys.
2. The thumb will play all the white keys except where two white keys are adjoining. The fingering is then 1-2 or 2-1 depending on which hand is playing. At no time should fingers 1 and 2 cross each other.

One octave Chromatic Scale fingering beginning on C:

 RH 1313 12 31313 12 / 21 31313 21 3131
 LH 1313 21 31313 21 / 12 31313 12 3131

APPENDIX IV - TWO-OCTAVE ARPEGGIOS BASIC FINGERING

RH - Root position: 1-2-3-1-2-3-5-3-2-1-3-2-1

 First inversion: 1-2-4-1-2-4-5-4-2-1-4-2-1

 Second inversion: 1-2-4-1-2-4-5-4-2-1-4-2-1

LH – Root position: 5-4-2-1-4-2-1-2-4-1-2-4-5

 First inversion: 5-4-2-1-4-2-1-2-4-1-2-4-5

 Second inversion: 5-3-2-1-3-2-1-2-3-1-2-3-5

The thumb does not play on the black keys. Alter fingerings to accommodate.

APPENDIX VIII – MAJOR AND MINOR SCALES

Major and Minor Scales

Major and Minor Scales

Major and Minor Scales